Charlton A

G000124420

Andy Croft

Published in association with The Basic Skills Agency

Hodder & Stoughton

A MEMBER OF THE HODDER HEADLINE GROUP

Acknowledgements

Cover:© Tom Morris

Photos: pp 2, 6, 8, 12, 14 Richard Redden/Club Heritage Committee; pp 16, 20, 23 Tom Morris

We are grateful to the Charlton Athletic Heritage Committee and to Richard Redden, author of the club history, *Valley of Tears, Valley of Joy*, for their help in preparing this book.

Every effort has been made to trace copyright holders of material reproduced in this book. Any rights not acknowledged will be acknowledged in subsequent printings if notice is given to the publisher.

Orders; please contact Bookpoint Ltd, 39 Milton Park, Abingdon, Oxon OX14 4TD. Telephone: (44) 01235 400414, Fax: (44) 01235 400454. Lines are open from 9.00–6.00, Monday to Saturday, with a 24 hour message answering service. Email address: orders@bookpoint.co.uk

British Library Cataloguing in Publication Data
A catalogue record for this title is available from the British Library

ISBN 0 340 77666 8

First published 2000
Impression number   10 9 8 7 6 5 4 3 2 1
Year   2005 2004 2003 2002 2001 2000

Typeset by GreenGate Publishing Services, Tonbridge, Kent.
Printed in Great Britain for Hodder and Stoughton Educational, a division of Hodder Headline Plc, 338 Euston Road, London NW1 3BH, by Redwood Books, Trowbridge, Wilts

Contents

Many people like Charlton Athletic.
They are a friendly club.
They always seem to play good football.

Once they were a top club.

They were one of the best teams in Britain.
They had the biggest ground.
They had very big crowds.

But that was a long time ago.

Lots of London clubs are in the Premiership.
Arsenal, Spurs, West Ham and Chelsea.

Now Charlton are joining them again,
back at the top where they belong.

1937 Charlton team

1 Did You Know?

Charlton are the only team to lose in the FA Cup
and still reach the FA Cup Final.
This was in 1946.
How did it happen?
It was the only time Cup games were played
over two legs.
Charlton beat Fulham in the first leg
of the third round
then lost to them in the second leg.

Charlton's ground is called The Valley.
It was built in an old chalk-pit.
They filled the pit with soil
from a local hospital.
The soil was full of human bones!

One of Charlton's most capped players
was John Hewie.
He was born in South Africa.
He played baseball for England.
He played football for Scotland.

Charlton once used three players in goal
in one game.
Not all at the same time!
Their goalie injured his finger.
Two outfield players took turns in goal.
They lost 11–1 to Aston Villa.

When Charlton played their first FA Cup Final
the ball burst.
Next season, when Charlton played in the
FA Cup Final
the ball burst again.

The first ever sub in the English League
was a Charlton player called Keith Peacock.

Charlton play at The Valley.
So they were sometimes called the Valiants.

They play in red and white.
So they were sometimes called the Robins.
Before home games
they still play the song,
The Red, Red Robin.

Their favourite name is the 'Addicks'.
After a game,
Charlton players used to eat fish and chips.
They went to a chip shop on East Street.
The owner was a Charlton fan.
He used to go to all the home matches.
He took an old haddock nailed to a piece of wood.
He used to wave it when Charlton scored.
That's why they are called the 'Addicks'.

Charlton have had eight different grounds so far.
They were thinking of moving
to the Millennium Dome
but now they are staying at The Valley.

The Valley in 1920.

2 Beginnings

The club was started in 1905
by some boys
who lived near the River Thames.
They called themselves Charlton Athletic.

They became one of the best little clubs in London.
In 1919 they joined the Kent League.
In 1920 they joined the Southern League.
In 1921 they joined the Third Division South.

They played in four different grounds.
Then they built a new stadium in 1919 .
They called it The Valley
because of its steep sides.

Four years later Charlton moved again.
They went to Catford.
But the fans were not happy.
The club soon went back to The Valley.

Jimmy Seed, Charlton's manager in 1933–1956, soon brought glory back to Charlton.

3 Glory Days

For 15 years Charlton did nothing.
They were just a little club from South London.

In 1933 Charlton had a new manager.
His name was Jimmy Seed.
He was a famous player.
He had played for some very big clubs.
He wanted to manage a little club.
He turned it into a big club.
Jimmy Seed was at Charlton for 23 years.

He didn't spend much money.
But he had some good scouts.
He soon built one of the best sides in the country:
Don Welsh,
George Tadman,
Harold Hobbis,
Sam Bartram.

Bartram played in goal.
He played 623 games for Charlton.
They once played Chelsea on a very foggy day.
It was so foggy the players could not see the goals.
The match was abandoned.
The players left the pitch.
The crowds went home.
But no-one told Sam Bartram.
He was still in goal!

In 1935 Charlton won the Third Division (South).
In 1936 they were second in the Second Division.
In 1937 they were second in the First Division.
In 1938 they were fourth.
In 1939 they were third.

The Valley was the biggest ground in the country.
There were big crowds there every week.
75,000 people saw Charlton play Villa
in the FA Cup.

Charlton were so good they even beat France.
France were supposed to play a friendly
against Italy.
Italy withdrew at the last moment.
So France asked Charlton instead.
Charlton beat Huddersfield 1–0 in the League.
The next day they went to Paris.
There they beat France 5–2!

1947 FA Cup team

4 Wembley

In 1946 Charlton reached the FA Cup final,
against Derby County.
Charlton's Bert Turner scored an own goal.
Then he equalised for Charlton.
He was the first player to score for both sides
in a Cup Final.
But Charlton lost 4–1.

The next season Charlton were back.
This time they were playing Burnley.
It was 0–0 for most of the match.
Six minutes before the end of extra time
Chris Duffy scored for Charlton.

Charlton had won something at last.

Jimmy Seed was very excited.
He dropped the FA Cup and broke the lid.

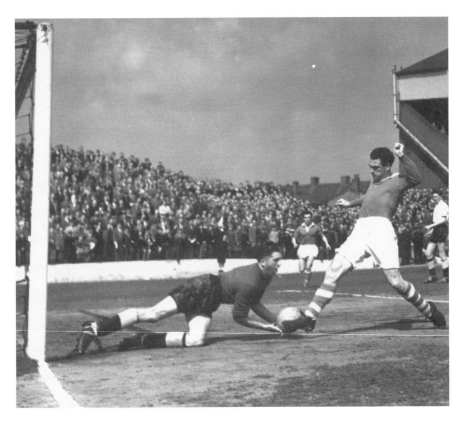

Johnny Summers in action.

5 An Amazing Game

In 1957 Charlton played Huddersfield
at home in the League.
It was one of the most amazing matches
ever played.

Huddersfield were winning 5–1.
Charlton were down to ten men.
There were only 28 minutes to go.

Then Charlton started to fight back.
They scored four goals.
Johnny Summers scored a hat-trick.
Charlton were level, 5–5.
Then Charlton scored another.
6–5 to Charlton.
Then Huddersfield equalised, 6–6.
So Charlton scored another.
Charlton won the game 7–6.

Johnny Summers scored five of Charlton's goals
that day.

What a game!

Allan Simonsen, European Footballer of the Year in February 1983.

6 Hard Times

In 1957 Charlton were relegated
to the Second Division.
They took 29 years to get back to the top.
They even spent four seasons
in the Third Division.

They tried to climb out of trouble.
But nothing seemed to go right.

They bought Allan Simonsen.
He was the European Footballer of the Year.
But Charlton could not afford his wages.
They had to sell him.

Charlton were broke.
They owed a lot of money.
A Nigerian chief tried to help the club.
They were almost closed down.
They were rescued with only 25 minutes to go.

But Charlton were still in big trouble.
They left The Valley.
They moved to Selhurst Park.
Then they moved to Upton Park.

But Charlton fans were unhappy.
They wanted to go back to The Valley.

In 1986 Lennie Lawrence took Charlton
back to the First Division.
They stayed up.
They hung on for four years.

Then they went down again.

7 Premiership

In 1991 Charlton chose two managers
to run the club – Alan Curbishley and Steve Gritt.
Both used to be Charlton players.

In 1992 Charlton moved back to The Valley,
back where they belonged.

Steve left but Alan stayed.
In 1998 he took the club to Wembley
for the First Division play-off final.
Charlton drew 4–4 with Sunderland.
It went to penalties.
Charlton won, 7–6.

Charlton were in the Premiership,
back where they belonged!

Alan Curbishley

They started well in the Premiership.
They even went top for a week.
Then they started slipping down the table.

Alan Curbishley tried hard.
The players tried hard.
Charlton played some good football.
They won lots of friends.
But it wasn't enough.

At the end of the season
Charlton were down again.

8 The Future

Charlton are now back
in the Premiership.
Will they be a yo-yo club
or can they stay up this time?

Alan Curbishley has the players:
Mark Kinsella,
Richard Rufus,
Dean Kiely,
Chris Powell
Andy Hunt.

But can they do it?
Will the great days come again to The Valley?

The 1999 Charlton team

Charlton are hoping to increase the size of The Valley.
They want to be a top club again.
Whatever happens,
Charlton fans will always sing their song:

'Many miles have I travelled,
Many games have I seen,
Following Charlton,
My favourite team,
Many hours have I spent
In the Covered End choir,
Singing Valley, Floyd Road,
My only desire.

Valley, Floyd Road,
O mist rolling in from the Thames,
My only desire is always to be
Down The Valley, Floyd Road.'

If you have enjoyed reading this book, you may be interested in other titles in the *Livewire* series.

Middlesbrough
Nottingham Forest
Sunderland
Wimbledon
Michael Owen
Alan Shearer
Tony Adams
Vinnie Jones
Ian Wright
Sheffield Wednesday
Derby County
Leeds United
Blackburn Rovers
West Ham United

Being a Striker
Being a Goalie
The World Cup